Mary and Jesus
in the Qur'ān

Reprinted from
The Meaning of the Holy Qur'ān
Translation and Commentary
by 'Abdullah Yūsuf 'Alī

amana publications

First Published

(1409 AH / 1989 AC: Amana Corp.)

Third Edition

(1415 AH / 1995AC)

Fourth Edition

(Revised and Expanded)

(1422 AH / 2002 AC)

Previously published under the title:
The Story of Mary and Jesus from the Qur'an

Library of Congress Cataloging-in-Publications Data

Koran, Sūrat Maryam, English & Arabic–
    The Story of Mary and Jesus from the Qur'an: reprinted from *The Meaning of the Holy Qur'an: New Edition with revised translation and commentary,* by Abdullah Yūsuf "Alī
    p. 32   cm   36 x 54
    Originally published: 1989.
    ISBN 0-915957-24-8
    1. Jesus Christ in the Koran.
    2. Mary, Blessed Virgin, Saint in the Koran.
    3. Alī, "Abdullah Yūsuf, 1872-1952. II. Title.
    297'. 1229–dc20

BP128.53.K56 1995   94-47660
                                                                    CIP
                                                                    NE

Printed in the United States of America by
International Graphics
10710 Tucker Street
Beltsville, Maryland 20705-2223 USA
Tel: (301) 595-5999   Fax: (301) 595-5888
E-mail: ig@igprinting.com
Website: igprinting.com

Introduction

The deference and esteem with which Muslims hold Jesus and his mother, peace be upon them, is readily manifest on reading the Qur'an.[1] *Sūrah* (Chapter) nineteenth of the Qur'an is named after *Maryam*, the Arabic name for Mary. The third *sūrah* of the Qur'an is titled *Āl 'Imrān* meaning The Family of 'Imrān (father of Moses). In these two chapters of the Qur'an the lives of the Virgin and her child, and before them of John the Baptist (Yaḥyā) are presented magnanimously in terms of compassion, grace, love, mercy and miracle.

Witness the verses that bring the good tidings of the coming birth of John the Baptist (Yaḥyā) and the Messiah (*Mesīḥ* in Arabic):

> ". . 0 Zakkariyya, We give thee
> Good news of a son:
> His name shall be Yaḥyā (John):
> On none by that name
> Have we conferred distinction before."
> He said, "0 my Lord!
> How shall I have a son,
> When my wife is barren
> And I have grown quite decrepit
> From old age?"
> He said: "So (it will be):
> Thy Lord saith, That is
> Easy for Me: I did
> Indeed create thee before,
> When thou hadst been nothing!" (19: 7-9)

and

> She (Mary) said: "How shall I
> Have a son, seeing that
> No man has touched me,
> And I am not unchaste?"
> He said: "So (it will be):
> Thy Lord saith, "That is
> Easy for Me: and
> (We Wish) to appoint him
> As a Sign unto men
> And a Mercy from Us:
> It is a matter (so) decreed." (19: 20-21)

Surah Maryam was revealed at a time when Prophet Muhammad and the new Makkan converts to Islam were being subject to increasing persecution for their belief in the Unity (Oneness) of God. Unable to ward off their plight, the Prophet asked them to migrate to other lands where they could find freedom of worship and live in peace. When asked as to where should they go, the Prophet advised them to escape to Abyssinia in Africa, a Christian kingdom –where "a king (the Negus) rules with justice, a land of truthfulness, until God leads us to a way out of our difficulty." Following the Prophet's advice, the first group of eleven Muslim men and women made their escape across the Red Sea to Abyssinia, soon to be followed by others. This migration to Abyssinia has come to be known in the annals of Islam as the *First Hijrah* (migration). At the time only forty seven Muslims remained in Makkah while those who sought freedom of worship in Abyssinia numbered over eighty.

Enraged by the flight of Muslims to Abyssinia, the Makkans immediately dispatched two of their distinguished emissaries, 'Amr ibn al 'As and Abdullah ibn Abu Rabi'ah to the Negus carrying precious gifts, to plead the extradition of the Muslims back to Makkah. The delegation presented their precious gifts to the Negus and his patriarch and made its case to have the Muslims extradited back to their homeland.

The Negus assembled his court and bishops and sent for the Muslim exiles. When all were assembled, the Negus addressed the Muslims: "What is this religion wherein you have become separate from your people, though you have not entered my religion nor that of any other folk that surround us?"

Ja'far ibn Abu Talib, the spokesman of the Muslims, answered him: "O King! We were a people steeped in ignorance, worshipping idols, eating unsacrificed carrion, committing abomination, and the strong among us would devour the weak. Thus, we were until God sent us a Messenger from our midst, one whose lineage, integrity, truthfulness, purity and veracity we knew well. He called us unto God, that we should testify to his Oneness and worship Him alone and renounce what we and our fathers had worshiped in the way of stones and idols; and he commanded us to speak truly, to fulfill our promises, to respect the ties of kinship and the rights of our neighbors, and to refrain from crimes and bloodshed. Therefore, we worship God alone, setting none beside Him, counting as forbidden what he has forbidden and as licit, what He has allowed. For these reasons our people have turned against us, and have persecuted us to make us forsake our religion and revert from the worship of God to the worship of idols. That is why we have come, seeking justice and protection, to your country, having chosen you above all others; and we hope, O King, that we shall not suffer wrong in your land."[2]

The Negus further asked the Muslims if they had with them any Revelation that their Prophet had brought them from God. When Ja'far answered that they had, he asked him to recite it. Ja'far recited the following passage from the *sūrah* of Mary, which had been revealed shortly before their flight to Abyssinia:

Relate in the Book
(The story of) Mary,
When she withdrew
From her family
To a pale in the East

She placed a screen
(To screen herself) from them;
Then We sent to her
Our Angel, and he appeared
Before her as a man
In all respects.

She said: " I seek refuge
From thee to (Allah)
Most Gracious: (come not near)
If thou dost fear Allah."

He said: "Nay, I am only
A messenger from thy Lord,
(To announce) to thee
The gift of a holy son."

She said: "How shall I
Have a son, seeing that
No man has touched me,
And I am not unchaste?"

He said: "So (it will be):
Thy Lord saith That is
Easy for Me: and (We
Wish) to appoint him

As a Sign unto men
And a Mercy from Us':
It is a matter
(So) decreed." (19: 16-21)

On hearing the recitation, the Negus and his bishops openly wept. He said: "This has truly come from the same source as that which Jesus brought." Addressing the two envoys of Quraysh he said: "You may leave, for by God I will not hand them over to you; they shall not be betrayed."

But the Quraysh delegation was not the one to give up that easily. They decided to use yet another ploy. They approached the Negus a second time claiming that Muslims aver that Jesus, the son of Mary is a slave. They told the Negus, "O King, they utter an enormous lie about Jesus the son of Mary. Do but send for them, and ask them what they say about Jesus." The Negus resummoned the Muslims to his court and inquired of them: "What do you say of Jesus, the son of Mary?" Ja'far answered with due reverence: "We say of him what our Prophet brought to us from Allah that he is the servant of God and His Messenger and His Spirit and His Word which He cast unto Mary the blessed virgin." The Negus picked up a piece of wood and said to those gathered: "Jesus the son of Mary exceeds not what you have said by the length of this stick." He then turned to the Muslims and said: "Go your ways, for you are safe in my land. Not for mountains of gold would I harm any one of you." Pointing to the envoys of Quraysh, he demanded his attendant to "return unto these two men their gifts, for I have no use for them." Thus, the envoys of Quraysh returned to Makkah empty-handed, their mission having failed while the Muslims stayed in peace in Abyssinia.

---

1. The sacred text of the Muslims, the Qur'an, has 114 *sūrahs* (chapters) of varying length, providing guidance to humankind on all aspects of life in this world and in the next. The Arabic text of the Qur'an comprises only the inscribed form of the revelation brought by the angel Gabriel (*Jibril* in Arabic) to Prophet Muhammad, may peace be upon him, during the twenty three years of his mission. The chapters in this volume are extracted from Abdullah Yusuf 'Ali's English translation of the Qur'an entitled *The Meaning of the Holy Qur'an* published by Amana Publications, Beltsville, Maryland, 1989. The reader may like to refer to that translation in order to follow up on information given in the footnotes by the translator.

2. Martin Lings, *Muhammad: his life based on the earliest sources*, Inner Traditions International, Rochester, Vermont, 1983, pp. 83-84.

5

Sūrah 19.

Maryam (Mary)

In the name of Allah, Most Gracious,
Most Merciful.

الجزءالسادس عشر ۝ سورة مريمر

بِسۡمِ ٱللَّهِ ٱلرَّحۡمَٰنِ ٱلرَّحِيمِ

1. K̲af H̲ā Y̲ā 'Ayn S̲ād.[2455]

كٓهيعٓصٓ ۝

2. (This is) a recital[2456]
Of the Mercy of thy Lord
To His Servant Zakarīyā.

ذِكۡرُ رَحۡمَتِ رَبِّكَ عَبۡدَهُۥ زَكَرِيَّآ ۝

3. Behold! he cried
To his Lord in secret,[2457]

إِذۡ نَادَىٰ رَبَّهُۥ نِدَآءً خَفِيًّا ۝

4. Praying: "O my Lord!
Infirm indeed are my bones,
And the hair of my head
Doth glisten with grey:
But never am I unblest,
O my Lord, in my prayer[2458]
To Thee!

قَالَ رَبِّ إِنِّي وَهَنَ ٱلۡعَظۡمُ مِنِّي
وَٱشۡتَعَلَ ٱلرَّأۡسُ شَيۡبًا
وَلَمۡ أَكُنۢ بِدُعَآئِكَ
رَبِّ شَقِيًّا ۝

5. "Now I fear (what)
My relatives (and colleagues)

وَإِنِّي خِفۡتُ ٱلۡمَوَٰلِيَ ۝

2455. This is the only Sūrah which begins with these five Abbreviated Letters, *Kāf, Hā, Yā, 'Ayn, Sād.*
For Abbreviated Letters generally, see Appendix I.

As stated in my note 25, such Letters are Symbols, of which the true meaning is known to Allah alone.
We should not be dogmatic about any conjectures that we make. According to the interpretation of the last
letter *Sād,* suggested in n. 989 to 7:1. I should be disposed to accept Sād with the meaning of *Qisas, i.e.,*
stories of the Prophets. The main figures referred to here are: Zakarīyā, Yahyā, Maryam, 'Īsā, and Ibrāhīm:
the others are mentioned but incidentally. The strong letter in ZaKarīyā is K; in IbrāHīm. H; in YāHYā and
perhaps MarYam, Y; and in 'Isa—'A ('Ayn). H also comes in Hārūn (Aaron), and the Arabic Yā' comes in
all the names including Ismā'īl and Idrīs.

I offer this suggestion with some diffidence. The suggestion of the *Tafsīr Kabīr* is that the letters stand
for attributes of Allah: K. for *Kafī* (the One sufficient in Himself); H. for *Hādī* (He who guides); Y. for *Yad*
(Hand as a symbol of Power and Authority; *Cf.* 48:10, "The Hand of Allah is above their hands"); 'A. for
'Alīm (the All-Knowing); and S for *Sādiq* (The True One).

2456. The Mercy of Allah to Zakarīyā was shown in many ways: (1) in the acceptance of his prayer; (2)
in bestowing a son like Yahyā; and (3) in the love between father and son, in addition to the work which
Yahyā did as Allah's Messenger for the world. *Cf.* 3:38-41 and notes. There the public ministry was the point
stressed; here the beautiful relations between the son and the father.

2457. *In secret:* because he feared that his own family and relatives were going wrong (19:5), and he wanted
to keep the lamp of Allah burning bright. He could not very well mention the fear about his colleagues (who
were his relations) in public.

2458. This preface shows the fervent faith of Zakarīyā. Zakarīyā was a priest of the Most High Allah.
His office was the Temple, and his relatives were his colleagues. But he found in them no true spirit of the
service of Allah and man. He was filled with anxiety as to who would uphold the godly ideas he had in mind,
which were strange to his worldly colleagues.

(Will do) after me:
But my wife is barren:
So give me an heir[2459]
As from Thyself—

مِن وَرَآءِى وَكَانَتِ ٱمْرَأَتِى عَاقِرًا
فَهَبْ لِى مِن لَّدُنكَ وَلِيًّا

6. "(One that) will (truly)
Represent me, and represent[2460]
The posterity of Jacob;
And make him, O my Lord!
One with whom Thou art
Well-pleased!"

٦ يَرِثُنِى وَيَرِثُ
مِنْ ءَالِ يَعْقُوبَ
وَٱجْعَلْهُ رَبِّ رَضِيًّا

7. (His prayer was answered):
"O ZakarĪyā! We give thee
Good news of a son:
His name shall be Yaḥyā:
On none by that name
Have We conferred distinction
before."[2461]

٧ يَٰزَكَرِيَّآ
إِنَّا نُبَشِّرُكَ بِغُلَٰمٍ ٱسْمُهُۥ يَحْيَىٰ
لَمْ نَجْعَل لَّهُۥ مِن قَبْلُ سَمِيًّا

8. He said: "O my Lord!
How shall I have a son,
When my wife is barren
And I have grown quite decrepit
From old age?"

٨ قَالَ رَبِّ أَنَّىٰ يَكُونُ لِى غُلَٰمٌ
وَكَانَتِ ٱمْرَأَتِى عَاقِرًا
وَقَدْ بَلَغْتُ مِنَ ٱلْكِبَرِ عِتِيًّا

9. He said: "So (it will be):[2462]
Thy Lord saith, 'That is
Easy for Me: I did

٩ قَالَ كَذَٰلِكَ قَالَ رَبُّكَ هُوَ عَلَىَّ هَيِّنٌ

2459. His was not merely a vulgar desire for a son. If it had been, he would have prayed much earlier in his life, when he was a young man. He was too full of true piety to put merely selfish things into his prayers. But here was a public need, in the service of the Lord. He was too old, but could he perhaps adopt a child—who would be an heir "as from Allah?" (See n. 380 to 3:38).

2460. It is true that an heir inherits property, but his higher duty is to represent in everything the personality of him from whom he inherits. It is doubtful whether ZakarĪyā had any worldly property. But he had character and virtue, as a man of God, and this he wanted to transmit to his heir as his most precious possession. It was almost the most precious possession of the posterity of Jacob. The people around him had fallen away from Allah's Message. Could his heir, like him, try and renew it?

2461. This was John the Baptist, the forerunner of Jesus. In accordance with his father's prayer he, and Jesus for whom he prepared the way, renewed the Message of Allah, which had been corrupted and lost among the Israelites. The Arabic form Yaḥyā suggests "Life". The Hebrew form is Johanan, which means "Jehovah has been Gracious". *Cf. Ḥanāna* in verse 13 below. It does not mean that the name was given for the first time, for we read of a Johanan the son of Careah in II Kings, 25:23, an otherwise obscure man. It means that Allah had, for the first time, called one of His elect by that name.

2462. Who is the "He" in this clause? As I have construed it, following the majority of Commentators, it means the angel who brought the message from Allah. *Cf.* 19:21 below. But some Commentators construe it to refer to ZakarĪyā. In that case the meaning will be: ZakarĪyā after a little reflection said (in his wonder) "So!", *i.e.* "Can it really be so? Can I really have a son in my old age?" The speech following, "Thy Lord saith," etc., will then be that of the angel-messenger.

Indeed create thee before,
When thou hadst been
　　　　　　　　　nothing!"[2463]

وَقَدْ خَلَقْتُكَ مِن قَبْلُ وَلَمْ تَكُ شَيْئًا

10. (Zakarīya) said: "O my Lord!
Give me a Sign."[2464]
"Thy Sign," was the answer,
"Shall be that thou
Shalt speak to no man
For three nights,[2465]
Although thou art not dumb."

قَالَ رَبِّ اجْعَل لِّى ءَايَةً
قَالَ ءَايَتُكَ أَلَّا تُكَلِّمَ النَّاسَ
ثَلَٰثَ لَيَالٍ سَوِيًّا

11. So Zakarīya came out
To his people
From his chamber:
He told them by signs
To celebrate Allah's praises
In the morning
And in the evening.

فَخَرَجَ عَلَىٰ قَوْمِهِۦ
مِنَ الْمِحْرَابِ فَأَوْحَىٰٓ إِلَيْهِمْ
أَن سَبِّحُوا بُكْرَةً وَعَشِيًّا

12. (To his son came the
　　　　　　command):[2466]
"O Yaḥyā! take hold
Of the Book with might":
And We gave him Wisdom[2467]
Even as a youth.

يَٰيَحْيَىٰ خُذِ
الْكِتَٰبَ بِقُوَّةٍ
وَءَاتَيْنَٰهُ الْحُكْمَ صَبِيًّا

2463. Every man was nothing just before he was created, *i.e.*, his personality was called into being by Allah. Even if there are material processes in forming the body, in accordance with the laws of nature, the real creative force is in Allah. But here there is a subtler meaning. John was the harbinger of Jesus, preparing the way for him: and this sentence also prepares us for the more wonderful birth of Jesus himself: see verse 21 below. Everything is possible with Allah.

2464. The "Sign", I understand, was not in order to convince Zakarīya that the Lord's promise was true, for he had faith; but it was a symbol by which he was to show in his conduct that he was to conform to his new destiny as the father of Yaḥyā who was to come. Yaḥyā was to take up the work, and Zakarīya was to be silent, although the latter was sound in body and there was nothing to prevent him from speaking.

2465. Compare this verse with 3:41. The variations are interesting. Here it is "for three nights": there it is "for three days". The meaning is the same, for a day is a period of 24 hours. But the point of view is different in each case. There it was from the point of view of the Ummah or Congregation, among whom he worked by day; here the point of view is that of his individual soul, which spent the nights in prayer and praise. Notice again that at the end of the next verse, we have here, "In the morning and in the evening", and at the end of 3:41, "In the evening and in the morning"—showing again that the point of view is reversed.

2466. Time passes. The son is born. In this section of the Sūrah the centre of interest is Yaḥyā, and the instruction is now given to him. 'Keep fast hold of Allah's revelation with all your might': for an unbelieving world had either corrupted or neglected it, and Yaḥyā (John the Baptist) was to prepare the way for Jesus, who was coming to renew and re-interpret it.

2467. *Ḥukm*, translated Wisdom, implies something more than Wisdom; it is the Wisdom or Judgement that is entitled to judge and command, as in the matter of denouncing sin.

13. And pity (for all creatures)
As from Us, and purity:²⁴⁶⁸
He was devout,

وَحَنَانًا مِّن لَّدُنَّا وَزَكَوٰةً وَكَانَ تَقِيًّا ۝

14. And kind to his parents,
And he was not overbearing
Or rebellious.

وَبَرًّا بِوَالِدَيْهِ وَلَمْ يَكُن جَبَّارًا عَصِيًّا ۝

15. So Peace on him
The day he was born,
The day that he dies,
And the day that he
Will be raised up
To life (again)!²⁴⁶⁹

وَسَلَٰمٌ عَلَيْهِ
يَوْمَ وُلِدَ وَيَوْمَ يَمُوتُ
وَيَوْمَ يُبْعَثُ حَيًّا ۝

C. 139. — Next comes the story of Jesus and his mother
(19:16-40.) Mary. She gave birth, as a virgin, to Jesus.
But her people slandered and abused her
As a disgrace to her lineage. Her son
Did defend her and was kind to her. He
Was a servant of Allah, a true Prophet,
Blessed in the gifts of Prayer and Charity,
But no more than a man: to call him
The son of Allah is to derogate from Allah's
Majesty, for Allah is High above all
His Creatures, the Judge of the Last Day.

SECTION 2.

16. Relate in the Book
(The story of) Mary,²⁴⁷⁰
When she withdrew
From her family
To a place in the East.²⁴⁷¹

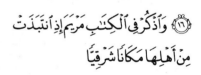

وَاذْكُرْ فِي الْكِتَٰبِ مَرْيَمَ إِذِ انتَبَذَتْ
مِنْ أَهْلِهَا مَكَانًا شَرْقِيًّا ۝

2468. John the Baptist did not live long. He was imprisoned by Herod, the tetrarch (provincial ruler under the Roman Empire), whom he had reproved for his sins, and eventually beheaded at the instigation of a woman with whom Herod was infatuated. But even in his young life, he was granted (1) wisdom by Allah, for he boldly denounced sin: (2) gentle pity and love for all Allah's creatures, for he moved among the humble and lowly, and despised "soft raiment": and (3) purity of life, for he renounced the world and lived in the wilderness. All his work he did in his youth. These things showed themselves in his conduct, for he was devout, showing love to Allah and to Allah's creatures, and more particularly to his parents (for we are considering that aspect of his life): this was also shown by the fact that he never used violence, from an attitude of arrogance, nor entertained a spirit of rebellion against divine Law. (R).

2469. This is spoken as in the lifetime of Yaḥyā. Peace and Allah's Blessings were on him when he was born; they continue when he is about to die an unjust death at the hands of a tyrant; and they will be specially manifest at the Day of Judgement.

2470. *Cf.* the story of Mary as related in 3:42-51. Here the whole theme is different: it is the personal side of the spiritual experiences of the worshippers of Allah in relation to their families or environment.

2471. To a private eastern chamber, perhaps in the Temple. She went into privacy, from her people and from people in general, for prayer and devotion. It was in this state of purity that the angel appeared to her in the shape of a man. She thought it *was* a man. She was frightened, and she adjured him not to invade her privacy.

17. She placed a screen
(To screen herself) from them;
Then We sent to her
Our angel, and he appeared
Before her as a man
In all respects.

١٧ فَٱتَّخَذَتْ مِن دُونِهِمْ حِجَابًا فَأَرْسَلْنَآ إِلَيْهَا رُوحَنَا فَتَمَثَّلَ لَهَا بَشَرًا سَوِيًّا

18. She said: "I seek refuge
From thee to (Allah)
Most Gracious: (come not near)
If thou dost fear Allah."

١٨ قَالَتْ إِنِّىٓ أَعُوذُ بِٱلرَّحْمَٰنِ مِنكَ إِن كُنتَ تَقِيًّا

19. He said: "Nay, I am only
A messenger from thy Lord,
(To announce) to thee
The gift of a holy son."[2472]

١٩ قَالَ إِنَّمَآ أَنَا۠ رَسُولُ رَبِّكِ لِأَهَبَ لَكِ غُلَٰمًا زَكِيًّا

20. She said: "How shall I
Have a son, seeing that
No man has touched me,
And I am not unchaste?"

٢٠ قَالَتْ أَنَّىٰ يَكُونُ لِى غُلَٰمٌ وَلَمْ يَمْسَسْنِى بَشَرٌ وَلَمْ أَكُ بَغِيًّا

21. He said: "So (it will be):
Thy Lord saith, 'That is
Easy for Me: and (We
Wish) to appoint him
As a Sign unto men
And a Mercy from Us':[2473]
It is a matter
(So) decreed."[2474]

٢١ قَالَ كَذَٰلِكِ قَالَ رَبُّكِ هُوَ عَلَىَّ هَيِّنٌ وَلِنَجْعَلَهُۥٓ ءَايَةً لِّلنَّاسِ وَرَحْمَةً مِّنَّا وَكَانَ أَمْرًا مَّقْضِيًّا

22. So she conceived him,
And she retired with him
To a remote place.[2475]

٢٢ فَحَمَلَتْهُ فَٱنتَبَذَتْ بِهِۦ مَكَانًا قَصِيًّا

2472. Allah had destined her to be the mother of the holy Prophet Jesus Christ, and now had come the time when this should be announced to her.

2473. The mission of Jesus is announced in two ways (1) he was to be a Sign to men; his wonderful birth and wonderful life were to turn an ungodly world back to Allah: and (2) his mission was to bring solace and salvation to the repentant. This, in some way or other, is the case with all prophets of Allah, and it was pre-eminently so in the case of the holy Prophet Muḥammad. But the point here is that the Israelites, to whom Jesus was sent, were a hardened race, for whom the message of Jesus was truly a gospel of Mercy.

2474. For anything that Allah wishes to create, He says "Be," and it is (*Cf.* 3:47). There is no interval between His decree and its accomplishment, except such as He imposes by His decree. Time may be only a projection of our own minds on this world of relativity.

2475. The annunciation and the conception, we may suppose, took place in Nazareth (of Galilee), say 65 miles north of Jerusalem. The delivery took place in Bethlehem about 6 miles south of Jerusalem. It was a remote place, not only with reference to the distance of 71 miles, but because in Bethlehem itself the birth was in an obscure corner under a palm tree, from which perhaps the babe was afterwards removed to a manger in a stable.

23. And the pains of childbirth
Drove her to the trunk
Of a palm tree:
She cried (in her anguish):
"Ah! would that I had
Died before this! would that
I had been a thing
Forgotten and out of sight!"[2476]

٢٣ فَأَجَاءَهَا
الْمَخَاضُ إِلَىٰ جِذْعِ النَّخْلَةِ
قَالَتْ يَٰلَيْتَنِى مِتُّ قَبْلَ هَٰذَا
وَكُنتُ نَسْيًا مَّنسِيًّا

24. But (a voice) cried to her
From beneath the (palm tree):
"Grieve not! for thy Lord
Hath provided a rivulet
Beneath thee;

٢٤ فَنَادَىٰهَا مِن تَحْتِهَا أَلَّا تَحْزَنِى
قَدْ جَعَلَ رَبُّكِ تَحْتَكِ سَرِيًّا

25. "And shake towards thyself
The trunk of the palm tree;
It will let fall
Fresh ripe dates upon thee.[2477]

٢٥ وَهُزِّى إِلَيْكِ بِجِذْعِ النَّخْلَةِ
تُسَٰقِطْ عَلَيْكِ رُطَبًا جَنِيًّا

26. "So eat and drink
And cool (thine) eye.[2478]
And if thou dost see
Any man, say, 'I have
Vowed a fast to (Allah)
Most Gracious, and this day
Will I enter into no talk
With any human being'"[2479]

٢٦ فَكُلِى وَاشْرَبِى وَقَرِّى عَيْنًا
فَإِمَّا تَرَيِنَّ مِنَ الْبَشَرِ أَحَدًا فَقُولِى
إِنِّى نَذَرْتُ لِلرَّحْمَٰنِ صَوْمًا
فَلَنْ أُكَلِّمَ الْيَوْمَ إِنسِيًّا

27. At length she brought
The (babe) to her people,
Carrying him (in her arms).
They said: "O Mary!

٢٧ فَأَتَتْ بِهِۦ قَوْمَهَا تَحْمِلُهُۥ
قَالُوا يَٰمَرْيَمُ

2476. She was but human, and suffered the pangs of an expectant mother, with no one to attend to her. The circumstances being peculiar, she had gotten far away from her people.

2477. Unseen Providence had seen that she should not suffer from thirst or from hunger. The rivulet provided her with water also for ablutions.

2478. *Cool thine eye*: An idiom for "comfort thyself and be glad". The literal meaning should not, however, be lost sight of. She was to cool her eyes (perhaps full of tears) with the fresh water of the rivulet and take comfort that a remarkable babe had been born to her. She was also to look around, and if any one came near, was to decline all conversation. It was quite true: she was under a vow, and could not talk to any one.

2479. She was to decline all conversation with man or woman, on the plea of a vow to Allah. The "fast" here does not mean abstinence literally from eating and drinking. She had just been advised to eat the dates and drink of the stream. It means abstinence from the ordinary household meals, and indeed from human intercourse generally.

سُورَةُ مَرْيَمَ   اَلْجُزْءُ السَّادِسَ عَشَرَ

Truly an amazing thing
Hast thou brought!²⁴⁸⁰

لَقَدْ جِئْتِ شَيْئًا فَرِيًّا

28. "O sister of Aaron!²⁴⁸¹
Thy father was not
A man of evil, nor thy
Mother a woman unchaste!"

٢٨ يَٰٓأُخْتَ هَٰرُونَ مَا كَانَ أَبُوكِ
ٱمْرَأَ سَوْءٍ وَمَا كَانَتْ أُمُّكِ بَغِيًّا

29. But she pointed to the babe.²⁴⁸²
They said: "How can we
Talk to one who is
A child in the cradle?"

٢٩ فَأَشَارَتْ إِلَيْهِ قَالُوا۟ كَيْفَ
نُكَلِّمُ مَن كَانَ فِى ٱلْمَهْدِ صَبِيًّا

30. He said: "I am indeed
A servant of Allah:
He hath given me
Revelation and made me
A prophet;

٣٠ قَالَ إِنِّى عَبْدُ ٱللَّهِ
ءَاتَىٰنِىَ ٱلْكِتَٰبَ وَجَعَلَنِى نَبِيًّا

31. "And He hath made me
Blessed wheresoever I be,
And hath enjoined on me
Prayer and Charity as long
As I live:²⁴⁸³

٣١ وَجَعَلَنِى مُبَارَكًا أَيْنَ مَا كُنتُ
وَأَوْصَٰنِى بِٱلصَّلَوٰةِ وَٱلزَّكَوٰةِ مَا دُمْتُ حَيًّا

32. "(He) hath made me kind
To my mother, and not
Overbearing or miserable;²⁴⁸⁴

٣٢ وَبَرًّۢا بِوَٰلِدَتِى
وَلَمْ يَجْعَلْنِى جَبَّارًا شَقِيًّا

2480. The amazement of the people knew no bounds. In any case they were ready to think the worst of her, as she disappeared from her kin for some time. But now she comes, shamelessly parading a babe in her arms! How she had disgraced the house of Aaron, the fountain of priesthood! We may suppose that the scene took place in the Temple in Jerusalem, or in Nazareth (*Cf.* 4:156).

2481. Aaron, the brother of Moses, was the first in the line of Israelite priesthood. Mary and her cousin Elisabeth (mother of Yaḥyā) came of a priestly family, and were therefore "sisters of Aaron" or daughters of 'Imrān (who was Aaron's father). See n. 375 to 3:35. Mary is reminded of her high lineage and the exceptional morals of her father and mother. How, they said, she had fallen, and disgraced the name of her progenitors!

2482. What could Mary do! How could she explain? Would they, in their censorious mood, accept her explanation? All she could do was to point to the child, who, she knew, was no ordinary child. And the child came to her rescue. By a miracle he spoke, defended his mother, and preached—to an unbelieving audience. See 3:46, and n. 388.

2483. There is a parallelism throughout the accounts of Jesus and Yaḥyā, with some variations. Both the parallelisms and the variations are interesting. For instance Jesus declares at the very outset that he is a servant of Allah, thus negativing the false notion that he was Allah or the son of Allah. The greatness of Yaḥyā is described in 19:12-13 in terms that are not applied to Jesus, but the verses 19:14-15 as applied to Yaḥyā are in almost identical terms with those applied to Jesus here (19:32-33). Devotion in Prayer and Charity is a good description of the Church of Christ at its best, and pity, purity, and devotion in Yaḥyā are a good description of the ways leading to Prayer and Charity, just as John led to Jesus.

2484. Overbearing violence is not only unjust and harmful to those on whom it is practised; it is perhaps even more harmful to the person who practises it, for his soul becomes turbid, unsettled, and ultimately unhappy and wretched—the state of those in Hell. Here the negative qualities are "not overbearing or miserable." As applied to John they were "not overbearing or rebellious." John bore his punishment from the State without any protest or drawing back.

33. "So Peace is on me
The day I was born,
The day that I die,
And the Day that I
Shall be raised up
To life (again)"!²⁴⁸⁵

(٣٣) وَٱلسَّلَـٰمُ عَلَىَّ يَوْمَ وُلِدتُّ
وَيَوْمَ أَمُوتُ
وَيَوْمَ أُبْعَثُ حَيًّا

34. Such (was) Jesus the son
Of Mary: (it is) a statement
Of truth, about which
They (vainly) dispute.²⁴⁸⁶

(٣٤) ذَٰلِكَ عِيسَى ٱبْنُ مَرْيَمَ
قَوْلَ ٱلْحَقِّ ٱلَّذِى فِيهِ يَمْتَرُونَ

35. It is not befitting
To (the majesty of) Allah
That He should beget
A son. Glory be to Him!
When He determines
A matter, He only says
To it, "Be," and it is.²⁴⁸⁷

(٣٥) مَا كَانَ لِلَّهِ أَن يَتَّخِذَ مِن وَلَدٍ
سُبْحَـٰنَهُۥٓ إِذَا قَضَىٰٓ أَمْرًا
فَإِنَّمَا يَقُولُ لَهُۥ كُن فَيَكُونُ

36. Verily Allah is my Lord
And your Lord: Him
Therefore serve ye: this is
A Way that is straight.²⁴⁸⁸

(٣٦) وَإِنَّ ٱللَّهَ رَبِّى وَرَبُّكُمْ فَٱعْبُدُوهُ
هَـٰذَا صِرَٰطٌ مُّسْتَقِيمٌ

37. But the sects differ
Among themselves: and woe
To the Unbelievers because
Of the (coming) Judgement²⁴⁸⁹
Of a momentous Day!

(٣٧) فَٱخْتَلَفَ ٱلْأَحْزَابُ مِنۢ بَيْنِهِمْ
فَوَيْلٌ لِّلَّذِينَ كَفَرُوا۟ مِن مَّشْهَدِ يَوْمٍ عَظِيمٍ

38. How plainly will they see
And hear, the Day that
They will appear before Us!

(٣٨) أَسْمِعْ بِهِمْ وَأَبْصِرْ يَوْمَ يَأْتُونَنَا

2485. *Cf.* 19:15, and n. 2469. Christ was not crucified (4:157). (R).

2486. The disputations about the nature of Jesus Christ were vain, but also persistent and sanguinary. The modern Christian churches have thrown them into the background, but they would do well to abandon irrational dogmas altogether.

2487. Begetting a son is a physical act depending on the needs of men's animal nature. Allah Most High is independent of all needs, and it is derogatory to Him to attribute such an act to Him. It is merely a relic of pagan and anthropomorphic materialist superstitions.

2488. As opposed to the crooked superstitions which take refuge in all sorts of metaphysical sophistries to prove three in one and one in three. In the Qur'ān there is no crookedness (18:1). Christ's teaching was simple, like his life, but the Christians have made it crooked.

2489. *Judgement*: the word in the original is *Mashhad*, which implies many things: (1) the time or place where evidence is taken, as in a Court of Judgement; (2) the time or place where people are produced (to be judged); and (3) the occasion for such production for the taking of evidence. A very expressive phrase for the Day of Judgement.

But the unjust today
Are in error manifest!²⁴⁹⁰

لَكِنِ ٱلظَّٰلِمُونَ ٱلْيَوْمَ فِى ضَلَٰلٍ مُّبِينٍ

39. But warn them of the Day
Of Distress,²⁴⁹¹ when
The matter will be determined:
For (behold), they are negligent
And they do not believe!

وَأَنذِرْهُمْ يَوْمَ ٱلْحَسْرَةِ إِذْ قُضِىَ ٱلْأَمْرُ وَهُمْ فِى غَفْلَةٍ وَهُمْ لَا يُؤْمِنُونَ

40. It is We Who will inherit²⁴⁹²
The earth, and all beings
Thereon: to Us will they
All be returned.

إِنَّا نَحْنُ نَرِثُ ٱلْأَرْضَ وَمَنْ عَلَيْهَا وَإِلَيْنَا يُرْجَعُونَ

C. 140. — Abraham pleaded with loving earnestness
(19:41-65.)   With his father to accept the truth of Allah:
He was turned out, but he retained
His gentleness and was blessed. Moses
Asked for the aid of his brother Aaron
And was true to his people. Ismā'īl
Was loyal to his father and his God, and was
A willing and accepted sacrifice to Allah.
Idrīs in his highest station held fast
To truth and integrity. Thus are the righteous
Shown true in their personal environment,
And inherit the Bliss in which the salutation
Is Peace — perfect Peace, the reward of the Constant.

SECTION 3.

41. (Also) mention in the Book
(The story of) Abraham:
He was a man of Truth.
A prophet.

وَٱذْكُرْ فِى ٱلْكِتَٰبِ إِبْرَٰهِيمَ إِنَّهُ كَانَ صِدِّيقًا نَّبِيًّا

42. Behold, he said to his father:²⁴⁹³
"O my father! why
Worship that which heareth not
And seeth not, and can
Profit thee nothing?

إِذْ قَالَ لِأَبِيهِ يَٰٓأَبَتِ لِمَ تَعْبُدُ مَا لَا يَسْمَعُ وَلَا يُبْصِرُ وَلَا يُغْنِى عَنكَ شَيْـًٔا

2490. *Cf.* 50:20-35, and that whole passage, where the Resurrection is described. (R).

2491. *Ḥasrah*: Sighs, sighing, regrets, distress.

2492. *Cf.* 3:180, n. 485; 15:23 n. 1964. Material property passes from one to another: when one dies another inherits it. Allah gives life and death, and all that survives after physical death goes back to Allah, the original source of all things (see also 19:20).

2493. The reference to Abraham here is in relation to his tender solicitude for his father, who had not received the light of Unity, and to whom Abraham wanted to be a guide and friend.

43. "O my father! to me
Hath come knowledge which
Hath not reached thee:[2494]
So follow me: I will guide
Thee to a Way that
Is even and straight.[2495]

44. "O my father! serve not
Satan: for Satan is
A rebel against (Allah)
Most Gracious.[2496]

45. "O my father! I fear
Lest a Penalty afflict thee[2497]
From (Allah) Most Gracious,
So that thou become
To Satan a friend."

46. (The father) replied: "Dost thou
Hate my gods, O Abraham?
If thou forbear not, I will
Indeed stone thee:
Now get away from me
For a good long while!"[2498]

47. Abraham said: "Peace be
On thee: I will pray
To my Lord for thy
forgiveness:[2499]

2494. Some are more receptive to Light than others. It is their duty and privilege to guide and point to the right Way.

2495. *Sawīyan*—right, smooth, even; complete, perfect; hence the derived meanings; in 19:10, 'in full possession of all the physical senses'; in that context, 'not dumb': in 19:17, when the angel appears in the form of a man, 'completely like' a man, a man 'in all respects.'

2496. The rebellion is all the more heinous and inexcusable, considering that Allah is Most Just, Most Merciful, Most Gracious.

2497. To entertain a feeling of friendliness, instead of aversion, to Evil, is in itself a degradation of our nature, a Penalty which Allah imposes on our deliberate rejection of the Truth. And the friendliness to Evil also implies the sharing of the outlawry of Evil.

2498. Note the gentle persuasive tone of Abraham in his speeches in 19:42-45 (for we may suppose those sentences to sum up a long course of arguments) and in 19:47-48, contrasted with the brusque and repellent tone of the father's reply in this verse. The one was the outcome of the true Light which had come to Abraham from Allah, as the other was the outcome of Pagan arrogance and the worship of brute force. The spiritual lesson from this episode of Abraham's life may be stated in four propositions: (1) the pious son is dutiful to his father and wishes him well in all things, material and spiritual; (2) if the father refuses Allah's Light, the son will do his utmost to bring such Light to the father; (3) having received the Light, the son will never renounce that Light, even if he has to forfeit his father's love and renounce his home; (4) even if the father repels him and turns him out, his answer will be a soft answer, full of love and forgiveness on the one hand, but firmness on behalf of Truth on the other.

2499. *Cf.* 9:114, where this promise of Abraham to pray for his father is referred to, and its limitations pointed out.

For He is to me
Most Gracious.

إِنَّهُۥ كَانَ بِى حَفِيًّا

48. "And I will turn away
From you (all) and from those
Whom ye invoke besides Allah:
I will call on my Lord:
Perhaps, by my prayer to my
Lord,
I shall be not unblest!"2500

وَأَعْتَزِلُكُمْ وَمَا تَدْعُونَ مِن دُونِ ٱللَّهِ وَأَدْعُوا۟ رَبِّى عَسَىٰٓ أَلَّآ أَكُونَ بِدُعَآءِ رَبِّى شَقِيًّا ٤٨

49. When he had turned away
From them and from those
Whom they worshipped besides
Allah, We bestowed on him
Isaac and Jacob, and each one
Of them We made a
prophet.2501

فَلَمَّا ٱعْتَزَلَهُمْ وَمَا يَعْبُدُونَ مِن دُونِ ٱللَّهِ وَهَبْنَا لَهُۥٓ إِسْحَٰقَ وَيَعْقُوبَ وَكُلًّا جَعَلْنَا نَبِيًّا ٤٩

50. And We bestowed
Of Our Mercy on them,
And We granted them
Lofty honour on the tongue2502
Of truth.

وَوَهَبْنَا لَهُم مِّن رَّحْمَتِنَا وَجَعَلْنَا لَهُمْ لِسَانَ صِدْقٍ عَلِيًّا ٥٠

SECTION 4.

51. Also mention in the Book
(The story of) Moses:
For he was specially chosen,
And he was a messenger
And a prophet.2503

وَٱذْكُرْ فِى ٱلْكِتَٰبِ مُوسَىٰٓ إِنَّهُۥ كَانَ مُخْلَصًا وَكَانَ رَسُولًا نَّبِيًّا ٥١

2500. Abraham left his father and the home of his fathers (Ur of the Chaldees) and never returned. He left because he was turned out, and because it was not possible for him to make any compromise with what was false in religion. In return for abuse, he spoke gentle words. And he expressed his fervent hope that at least he (Abraham) would have Allah's blessing in reply to his prayers. Here was a prefiguration of another Hijrah many centuries later! In both cases the prayer was abundantly fulfilled.

2501. Isaac and Isaac's son Jacob are mentioned here as carrying on one line of Abraham's traditions. The other line was carried on by Ismā'īl, who is mentioned independently five verses lower down, as his line got special honour in the Holy Prophet of Islam. That is why his mention comes after that of Moses *Cf.* 21:72.

2502. Abraham and his son and grandson Isaac and Jacob, and their line, maintained the banner of Allah's spiritual truth for many generations, and they won deservedly high praise—the praise of truth—on the tongues of men. Abraham prayed that he should be praised by the tongue of truth among men to come in later ages: 26:84. Ordinary praise may mean nothing: it may be due to self-flattery on the part of others or artful management by the person praised. Praise on the tongue of sincere truth is praise indeed!

2503. Moses was (1) especially chosen, and therefore prepared and instructed in all the wisdom of the Egyptians, in order that he might free his people from Egyptian bondage; there may also be a reference to Moses's title of *Kalīm Allah*, the one to whom Allah spoke without the intervention of angels: see 4:164, and n. 670); (2) he was a prophet (*nabī*), in that he received inspiration; and (3) he was a messenger (*rasūl*) in that he had a Book of Revelation, and an Ummah or organised Community, for which he instituted laws. (R).

52. And We called him
From the right side[2504]
Of Mount (Sinai), and made
Him draw near to Us,
For mystic (converse).

53. And, out of Our Mercy,[2505]
We gave him his brother
Aaron, (also) a prophet.

54. Also mention in the Book
(The story of) Ismā'īl:
He was (strictly) true
To what he promised,[2506]
And he was a messenger
(And) a prophet.

55. He used to enjoin
On his people Prayer
And Charity, and he was
Most acceptable in the sight
Of his Lord.[2507]

56. Also mention in the Book
The case of Idrīs:[2508]

2504. The incident here I think refers to the incidents described more fully in 20:9-36; a reference may also be made to Exod. 3:1-18 and 4:1-17. The time is when Moses (with his family) was travelling and grazing the flocks of his father-in-law Jethro, just before he got his commission from Allah. The place is somewhere near Mount Sinai (*Jabal Mūsā*). Moses sees a Fire in the distance, but when he goes there, he hears a voice that tells him it is sacred ground. Allah asked him to put off his shoes and to draw near, and when he went near, great mysteries were revealed to him. He was given his commission, and his brother Aaron was given to him to go with him and aid him. It is after that that he and Aaron went and faced Pharaoh in Egypt, as narrated in 7:103-144, etc. The *right side* of the mountain may mean that Moses heard the voice from the right side of the mountain as he faced it: or it may have the figurative meaning of "right" in Arabic, *i.e.*, the side which was blessed or sacred ground (see also 20:80). (R).

2505. Moses was diffident, and reluctant to go to Pharaoh as he had an impediment in his tongue, and he asked that his brother Aaron should be associated with him in his mission. Allah in His Mercy granted his request: 20:25-36.

2506. Ismā'īl was *Dhabīh Allah*, *i.e.*, the chosen sacrifice of Allah in Muslim tradition. When Abraham told him of the sacrifice, he voluntarily offered himself for it, and never flinched from his promise, until the sacrifice was redeemed by the substitution of a ram under Allah's commands. He was the fountainhead of the Arabian Ummah, and in his posterity came the Prophet of Allah. The Ummah and the Book of Islam reflect back the prophethood on Ismā'īl.

2507. An acceptable sacrifice: see last note.

2508. Idrīs is mentioned twice in the Qur'ān, *viz.*: here and in 21:85, where he is mentioned among those who patiently preserved His identification with the Biblical Enoch, who "walked with God" (Gen. 5:21-24), may or may not be correct. Nor are we justified in interpreting verse 57 here as meaning the same thing as in Gen. 5:24 ("God took him"), that he was taken up without passing through the portals of death. All we are told is that he was a man of truth and sincerity, and a prophet, and that he had a high position among his people. It is this point which brings him in the series of men just mentioned: he kept himself in touch with his people, and was honoured among them. Spiritual progress need not cut us off from our people, for we have to help and guide them. He kept to truth and piety in the highest station.

He was a man of truth
(And sincerity), (and) a prophet:

إِنَّهُ كَانَ صِدِّيقًا نَّبِيًّا

57. And We raised him
To a lofty station.

﴿٥٧﴾ وَرَفَعْنَهُ مَكَانًا عَلِيًّا

58. Those were some
Of the prophets on whom
Allah did bestow His Grace—
Of the posterity of Adam,
And of those whom We
Carried (in the Ark)
With Noah, and of
The posterity of Abraham[2509]
And Israel—of those
Whom We guided and chose;
Whenever the Signs
Of (Allah) Most Gracious
Were rehearsed to them,[2510]
They would fall down
In prostrate adoration
And in tears.

﴿٥٨﴾ أُوْلَئِكَ الَّذِينَ أَنْعَمَ اللَّهُ عَلَيْهِم
مِّنَ النَّبِيِّنَ مِن ذُرِّيَّةِ ءَادَمَ
وَمِمَّنْ حَمَلْنَا مَعَ نُوحٍ
وَمِن ذُرِّيَّةِ إِبْرَهِيمَ وَإِسْرَءِيلَ
وَمِمَّنْ هَدَيْنَا وَاجْتَبَيْنَا
إِذَا تُتْلَى عَلَيْهِمْ ءَايَتُ الرَّحْمَنِ
خَرُّوا سُجَّدًا وَبُكِيًّا

59. But after them there followed
A posterity who missed
Prayers and followed after lusts:
Soon, then, will they
Face Destruction—[2511]

﴿٥٩﴾ فَخَلَفَ مِنْ بَعْدِهِمْ خَلْفٌ أَضَاعُوا الصَّلَوةَ
وَاتَّبَعُوا الشَّهَوَاتِ فَسَوْفَ يَلْقَوْنَ غَيًّا

60. Except those who repent
And believe, and work
Righteousness: for these
Will enter the Garden
And will not be wronged
In the least—

﴿٦٠﴾ إِلَّا مَن تَابَ وَءَامَنَ وَعَمِلَ
صَلِحًا فَأُوْلَئِكَ يَدْخُلُونَ الْجَنَّةَ
وَلَا يُظْلَمُونَ شَيْئًا

61. Gardens of Eternity, those
Which (Allah) Most Gracious
Has promised to His servants

﴿٦١﴾ جَنَّتِ عَدْنٍ الَّتِي وَعَدَ الرَّحْمَنُ عِبَادَهُ

2509. The earlier generations are grouped into three epochs from a spiritual point of view: (1) from Adam to Noah, (2) from Noah to Abraham, and (3) from Abraham to an indefinite time, say to the time when the Message of Allah was corrupted and the need arose for the final Messenger of Unity and Truth. Israel is another name for Jacob.

2510. The original is in the Aorist tense, implying that the "Posterity" alluded to includes not only the messengers but their worthy followers who are true to Allah and uphold His standard.

2511. This selfish godless posterity gains the upper hand at certain times but, even then there is always a minority who see the error of their ways, repent and believe, and live righteous lives. They are not penalised in the Hereafter because they were associated with the ungodly in time. They reap the full reward of their faith and righteousness.

الجزءالسادس عشر   سُورَةُ مَرْيَم

In the Unseen: for His promise
Must (necessarily) come to pass.

بِٱلْغَيْبِ إِنَّهُ كَانَ وَعْدُهُ مَأْتِيًّا

62. They will not there hear
Any vain discourse, but
Only salutations of Peace:[2512]
And they will have therein
Their sustenance,[2313] morning
And evening.

۝ لَّا يَسْمَعُونَ فِيهَا لَغْوًا إِلَّا سَلَٰمًا
وَلَهُمْ رِزْقُهُمْ فِيهَا
بُكْرَةً وَعَشِيًّا

63. Such is the Garden which
We give as an inheritance
To those of Our Servants
Who guard against evil.

۝ تِلْكَ ٱلْجَنَّةُ ٱلَّتِى نُورِثُ مِنْ
عِبَادِنَا مَن كَانَ تَقِيًّا

64. (The angels say:)[2514]
"We descend not but
By command of thy Lord:
To Him belongeth what is
Before us, and what is
Behind us, and what is
Between: and thy Lord
Never doth forget"—

۝ وَمَا نَتَنَزَّلُ إِلَّا بِأَمْرِ رَبِّكَ
لَهُۥ مَا بَيْنَ أَيْدِينَا
وَمَا خَلْفَنَا وَمَا بَيْنَ ذَٰلِكَ
وَمَا كَانَ رَبُّكَ نَسِيًّا

65. "Lord of the heavens
And of the earth,
And of all that is
Between them: so worship Him,
And be constant and patient
In His worship: knowest thou
Of any who is worthy
Of the same Name as He?"[2515]

۝ رَّبُّ ٱلسَّمَٰوَٰتِ وَٱلْأَرْضِ
وَمَا بَيْنَهُمَا فَٱعْبُدْهُ
وَٱصْطَبِرْ لِعِبَٰدَتِهِۦ
هَلْ تَعْلَمُ لَهُۥ سَمِيًّا

2512. *Salām*, translated "Peace", has a much wider signification. It includes (1) a sense of security and permanence, which is unknown in this life; (2) soundness, freedom from defects, perfection, as in the word *salīm*; (3) preservation, salvation, deliverance, as in the word *sallama*; (4) salutation, accord with those around us; (5) resignation, in the sense that we are satisfied and not discontented; besides (6) the ordinary meaning of Peace, *i.e.*, freedom from any jarring element. All these shades of meaning are implied in the word *Islām*. (R).

2513. *Rizq*: literally sustenance or means of subsistence, the term covers all the means of perfect satisfaction of the body and soul. Morning and evening *i.e.*, early and late, all the time, always. (R).

2514. We are apt to be impatient of the evils we see around us. We may give of our best service to Allah, and yet see no results. In our human short-sightedness we may complain within ourselves. But we must not be impatient. The angels of Grace come not haphazardly, but by command of Allah according to His Universal Will and Purpose. Allah does not forget. If things are delayed, it is in accordance with a wise providence, which cares for all. Our plain duty is to be patient and constant in His service. (R).

2515. The more we taste of the truth and mystery of life, the more do we realise that there is no one to be mentioned in the same breath as Allah. He is above all names. But when we think of His beautiful qualities, and picture them to ourselves by names which give us some ideas of Him, we can search the whole wide world of our imagination, and we shall not find another to be compared with Him in name or quality. He is the One: praise be to Him!

C. 141. — Why should man disbelieve in the Hereafter?
(19:66-98.)   We all must pass through the fire of temptation.
But Allah Most Gracious will save us
If we accept Him and do right. Sin
May have its respite, but must run
To its own destruction. We must not
Dishonour Allah by holding false
And monstrous ideas of Him. Glory
To Him that He cares for all His creatures!

SECTION 5.

66. Man says: "What!
When I am dead, shall I
Then be raised up alive?"

٦٦ وَيَقُولُ ٱلْإِنسَـٰنُ أَءِذَا مَا مِتُّ
لَسَوْفَ أُخْرَجُ حَيًّا

67. But does not man
Call to mind that We
Created him before
Out of nothing?

٦٧ أَوَلَا يَذْكُرُ ٱلْإِنسَـٰنُ
أَنَّا خَلَقْنَـٰهُ مِن قَبْلُ وَلَمْ يَكُ شَيْـًٔا

68. So, by thy Lord,
Without doubt, We shall gather
Them together, and (also)
The Evil Ones (with them);[2516]
Then shall We bring them
Forth on their knees
Round about Hell;[2517]

٦٨ فَوَرَبِّكَ لَنَحْشُرَنَّهُمْ
وَٱلشَّيَـٰطِينَ ثُمَّ لَنُحْضِرَنَّهُمْ
حَوْلَ جَهَنَّمَ جِثِيًّا

69. Then shall We certainly
Drag out from every sect
All those who were worst
In obstinate rebellion
Against (Allah) Most Gracious.

٦٩ ثُمَّ لَنَنزِعَنَّ مِن كُلِّ شِيعَةٍ
أَيُّهُمْ أَشَدُّ عَلَى ٱلرَّحْمَـٰنِ عِتِيًّا

70. And certainly We know best
Those who are most worthy
Of being burned therein.

٧٠ ثُمَّ لَنَحْنُ أَعْلَمُ بِٱلَّذِينَ
هُمْ أَوْلَىٰ بِهَا صِلِيًّا

2516. The disbelief in a future state is not merely a philosophic doubt, but a warped will, a disingenuous obstinacy in face of our inner spiritual instincts and experiences. We were nothing before. Cannot the same Allah who created us out of nothing also continue our personality? But if we refuse to accept His light and guidance, our state will grow worse and worse. We shall be deprived of His grace. We shall be herded with the Evil Ones. In utter humiliation we shall be faced with all the consequences of our refusal of Truth.

2517 *Round about Hell*: There are many ways leading to evil, and people get to it from all round. Hence the mention of the seven Gates of Hell: see 15:44, and n. 1977. (R).

71. Not one of you but will[2518]
Pass over it: this is,
With thy Lord, a Decree
Which must be accomplished.

۞ وَإِن مِّنكُمْ إِلَّا وَارِدُهَا ۚ كَانَ عَلَىٰ رَبِّكَ حَتْمًا مَّقْضِيًّا ٧١

72. But We shall save those
Who guarded against evil,
And We shall leave
The wrongdoers therein,
(Humbled) to their knees.

۞ ثُمَّ نُنَجِّي الَّذِينَ اتَّقَوا وَّنَذَرُ الظَّالِمِينَ فِيهَا جِثِيًّا ٧٢

73. When Our Clear Signs
Are rehearsed to them,
The Unbelievers say to those
Who believe, "Which of the two
Sides is best in point of
Position? which makes the best
Show in Council?"[2519]

۞ وَإِذَا تُتْلَىٰ عَلَيْهِمْ ءَايَٰتُنَا بَيِّنَٰتٍ قَالَ الَّذِينَ كَفَرُوا لِلَّذِينَ ءَامَنُوٓا أَيُّ الْفَرِيقَيْنِ خَيْرٌ مَّقَامًا وَأَحْسَنُ نَدِيًّا ٧٣

74. But how many (countless)
Generations before them
Have We destroyed,
Who were even better
In equipment and in glitter
To the eye?

۞ وَكَمْ أَهْلَكْنَا قَبْلَهُم مِّن قَرْنٍ هُمْ أَحْسَنُ أَثَٰثًا وَرِءْيًا ٧٤

75. Say: "If any man go
Astray, (Allah) Most Gracious
Extends (the rope) to them.
Until, when they see
The warning of Allah (being
Fulfilled)—either in punishment[2520]
Or in (the approach of)
The Hour—they will
At length realise who is

۞ قُلْ مَن كَانَ فِي الضَّلَٰلَةِ فَلْيَمْدُدْ لَهُ الرَّحْمَٰنُ مَدًّا ۚ حَتَّىٰ إِذَا رَأَوْا مَا يُوعَدُونَ إِمَّا الْعَذَابَ وَإِمَّا السَّاعَةَ فَسَيَعْلَمُونَ مَنْ هُوَ ٧٥

2518. Three interpretations are possible: (1) The general interpretation is that every soul must pass through or by or over the Fire. Those who have had *Taqwā* (see n. 26 to 2:2) will be saved by Allah's Mercy, while unrepentant sinners will suffer the torments in ignominy. (2) If we refer the pronoun "you" to those "in obstinate rebellion" in verse 69 above, both leaders and followers in sin, this verse only applies to the wicked. (3) Some refer this verse to the Bridge over Hell, the Bridge *Sirāt*, over which all must pass to their final Destiny. This Bridge is not mentioned in the Qur'ān. (R).

2519. The Unbelievers may, for a time, make a better show in worldly position, or in people's assemblages where things are judged by the counting of heads. But Truth must prevail even in this world, and ultimately the positions must be reversed.

2520. Allah's warning is that every evil deed must have its punishment, and that there will be a Hereafter, the Day of Judgement, or the Hour, as it is frequently called. The punishment of evil often begins in this very life. For instance, over-indulgence and excesses of all kinds bring on their Nemesis quite soon in this very life. But some subtler forms of selfishness and sin will be punished—as every evil will be punished—in its own good time, as the Hour approaches. In either case, the arrogant boasting sinners will realise that their taunt—who is best in position and in forces? (19:73)—is turned against themselves.

Worst in position, and (who is)
Weakest in forces!

شَرٌّ مَّكَانًا وَأَضْعَفُ جُندًا ۞

76. "And Allah doth advance
In guidance those who seek
Guidance: and the things
That endure. Good Deeds,
Are best in the sight
Of thy Lord, as rewards,
And best in respect of
(There) eventual returns." [2521]

۞ وَيَزِيدُ اللّٰهُ الَّذِينَ اهْتَدَوْا هُدًى ۗ
وَالْبَاقِيَاتُ الصَّالِحَاتُ خَيْرٌ
عِندَ رَبِّكَ ثَوَابًا وَخَيْرٌ مَّرَدًّا

77. Hast thou then seen
The (sort of) man who
Rejects Our Signs, yet
Says: "I shall certainly
Be given wealth and children?" [2522]

۞ أَفَرَءَيْتَ الَّذِى كَفَرَ بِـَٔايَـٰتِنَا
وَقَالَ لَأُوتَيَنَّ مَالًا وَوَلَدًا

78. Has he penetrated to
The Unseen, or has he
Taken a contract with
(Allah) Most Gracious?

۞ أَطَّلَعَ الْغَيْبَ أَمِ اتَّخَذَ
عِندَ الرَّحْمَـٰنِ عَهْدًا

79. Nay! We shall record
What he says, and We
Shall add and add
To his punishment. [2523]

۞ كَلَّا ۚ سَنَكْتُبُ مَا يَقُولُ
وَنَمُدُّ لَهُۥ مِنَ الْعَذَابِ مَدًّا

80. To Us shall return [2524]
All that he talks of,
And he shall appear
Before Us bare and alone.

۞ وَنَرِثُهُۥ مَا يَقُولُ
وَيَأْتِينَا فَرْدًا

81. And they have taken
(For worship) gods other than

۞ وَاتَّخَذُوا مِن دُونِ اللّٰهِ ءَالِهَةً

2521. These lines are the same as in 18:46 (second clause), (where see n. 2387), except that the word *maradda* (eventual returns) is here subsituted for *amal* (hope). The meaning is practically the same: but "hope" is more appropriate in the passage dealing with this world's goods, and "eventual returns" in the passage dealing with sinner's specific investments and commitments in worldly position and organised cliques.

2522. Besides the man who boasts of wealth and power in actual possession, there is a type of man who boasts of getting them in the future and builds his worldly hopes thereon. Is he sure? He denies Allah, and His goodness and Mercy. But all good is in the hands of Allah. Can such a man then bind Allah to bless him when he rejects faith in Allah? Or does he pretend that he has penetrated the mysteries of the future? For no man can tell what the future holds for him.

2523. Such a man deserves double punishment—for rejecting Allah, and for his blasphemies with His Holy Name.

2524. Literally, "We shall inherit", *Cf.* 19:40 and n. 2492. Even if the man had property and power, it must go back to the source of all things, and the man must appear before the Judgement Seat, alone and unaccompanied, stripped of all the things from which he expected so much!

Allah, to give them
Power and glory!²⁵²⁵

82. Instead, they shall reject
Their worship, and become
Adversaries against them.²⁵²⁶

SECTION 6.

83. Seest thou not that We
Have set the Evil Ones on
Against the Unbelievers,
To incite them with fury?²⁵²⁷

84. So make no haste
Against them, for We
But count out to them
A (limited) number (of days).

85. The day We shall gather
The righteous to (Allah)
Most Gracious, like a band
Presented before a king for
honours.

86. And We shall drive
The sinners to hell,
Like thirsty cattle
Driven down to water—²⁵²⁸

87. None shall have the power
Of intercession, but such a one
As has received permission
(or promise)
From (Allah) Most Gracious.

2525. *'Izza* = exalted rank, power, might, the ability to impose one's will or to carry out one's will.

2526. *Cf.* 10:28-30, where the idols deny that they knew anything of their worship, and leave their worshippers in the lurch; and 5:116, where Jesus denies that he asked for worship, and leaves his false worshippers to the punishment or the mercy of Allah.

2527. Under the laws instituted by Allah, when evil reaches a certain stage of rebellion and defiance, it is left to gather momentum and to rush with fury to its own destruction. It is given a certain amount of respite, as a last chance: but failing repentance, its days are numbered. The godly therefore should not worry themselves over the apparent worldly success of evil, but should get on with their own duties in a spirit of trust in Allah.

2528. Note the contrast between the saved and the doomed. The one march with dignity like honoured ones before a king, and the other rush in anguish to their punishment like a herd of cattle driven down by thirst to their watering place. Note the metaphor of the water. They rush madly for water but are plunged into the Fire!

88. They say: "(Allah) Most
                Gracious
Has begotten a son!"

٨٨ وَقَالُواْ ٱتَّخَذَ ٱلرَّحْمَٰنُ وَلَدًا

89. Indeed ye have put forth
A thing most monstrous![2529]

٨٩ لَّقَدْ جِئْتُمْ شَيْئًا إِدًّا

90. As if the skies are ready
To burst, the earth
To split asunder, and
The mountains to fall down
In utter ruin.

٩٠ تَكَادُ ٱلسَّمَٰوَٰتُ يَتَفَطَّرْنَ مِنْهُ
وَتَنشَقُّ ٱلْأَرْضُ وَتَخِرُّ ٱلْجِبَالُ هَدًّا

91. That they should invoke
A son for (Allah) Most
                Gracious.

٩١ أَن دَعَوْاْ لِلرَّحْمَٰنِ وَلَدًا

92. For it is not consonant
With the majesty of (Allah)
Most Gracious that He
Should beget a son.[2530]

٩٢ وَمَا يَنۢبَغِى لِلرَّحْمَٰنِ
أَن يَتَّخِذَ وَلَدًا

93. Not one of the beings
In the heavens and the earth
But must come to (Allah)
Most Gracious as a servant.

٩٣ إِن كُلُّ مَن فِى ٱلسَّمَٰوَٰتِ وَٱلْأَرْضِ
إِلَّآ ءَاتِى ٱلرَّحْمَٰنِ عَبْدًا

94. He does take an account
Of them (all), and hath
Numbered them (all)
                exactly.[2531]

٩٤ لَّقَدْ أَحْصَىٰهُمْ
وَعَدَّهُمْ عَدًّا

95. And every one of them
Will come to Him singly
On the day of Judgement.

٩٥ وَكُلُّهُمْ ءَاتِيهِ يَوْمَ ٱلْقِيَٰمَةِ فَرْدًا

96. On those who believe
And work deeds of
                righteousness,

٩٦ إِنَّ ٱلَّذِينَ ءَامَنُواْ وَعَمِلُواْ
ٱلصَّٰلِحَٰتِ

2529. The belief in Allah begetting a son is not a question of words or of speculative thought. It is a stupendous blasphemy against Allah. It lowers Allah to the level of an animal. If combined with the doctrine of vicarious atonement, it amounts to a negation of Allah's justice and man's personal responsibility. It is destructive of all moral and spiritual order, and is condemned in the strongest possible terms.

2530. This basic principle was laid down early in the argument (19:35). It was illustrated by a reference to the personal history of many messengers, including Jesus himself, who behaved justly as men to their kith and kin and humbly served Allah. The evil results of such superstitions were pointed out in the case of many previous generations which went to their ruin by dishonouring Allah. And the argument is now rounded off towards the close of the Sūrah.

2531. Allah has no sons or favourites or parasites, such as we associate with human beings. On the other hand every creature of His gets His love, and His cherishing care. Every one of them, however humble, is individually marked before His Throne of Justice and Mercy, and will stand before Him on his own deserts.

Will (Allah) Most Gracious
Bestow Love.[2532]

سَيَجْعَلُ لَهُمُ الرَّحْمَنُ وُدًّا

97. So have We made
The (Qur'ān) easy
In thine own tongue,
That with it thou mayest give
Glad tidings to the righteous,
And warnings to people
Given to contention.

﴿٩٧﴾ فَإِنَّمَا يَسَّرْنَهُ بِلِسَانِكَ
لِتُبَشِّرَ بِهِ الْمُتَّقِينَ
وَتُنذِرَ بِهِ قَوْمًا لُّدًّا

98. But how many (countless)
Generations before them[2533]
Have We destroyed? Canst thou
Find a single one of them
(Now) or hear (so much
As) a whisper of them?

﴿٩٨﴾ وَكَمْ أَهْلَكْنَا قَبْلَهُم
مِّن قَرْنٍ هَلْ تُحِسُّ مِنْهُم مِّنْ أَحَدٍ
أَوْ تَسْمَعُ لَهُمْ رِكْزًا

2532. His own love, and the love for man's fellow creatures, in the world and in the Hereafter. Goodness breeds love and peace, and sin breeds hatred and contention.

2533. *Cf.* 19:74, from which this sentence is brought up as a reminiscence, showing the progress of sin, the Guidance which Allah gives to the good, the degradation of blasphemy, the respite granted, and the final End, when personal responsibility will be enforced.

Sūrah 3.

Āl 'Imrān (The Family of 'Imrān)

In the name of Allah, Most Gracious,
Most Merciful.

1. Alif Lām Mīm.

2. Allah! There is no god
But He—the Living,
The Self-Subsisting, Eternal.

3. It is He Who sent down
To thee (step by step),
In truth, the Book,
Confirming what went before it;
And He sent down the Law
(Of Moses) and the Gospel
(Of Jesus) ....

SECTION 4.

31. Say: "If ye do love Allah,
Follow me: Allah will love you
And forgive you your sins;
For Allah is Oft-Forgiving,
Most Merciful."

32. Say: "Obey Allah
And His Messenger":
But if they turn back,
Allah loveth not those
Who reject Faith.

33. Allah did choose
Adam and Noah, the family
Of Abraham, and the family
Of 'Imrān above all people—

34. Offspring, one of the other;[374]
And Allah heareth
And knoweth all things.

---

374. The Prophets in the Jewish-Christian-Muslim dispensation form one family literally. But the argument
is wider. All men of God form spiritually one family. If you love and obey Allah, love and obey His Messenger;
your love, obedience, and discipline will be the test of your faith.

35. Behold! a woman of 'Imrān[375]
Said: "O my Lord! I do
Dedicate unto Thee
What is in my womb
For Thy special service:[376]
So accept this of me:
For Thou hearest
And knowest all things."

۞ إِذْ قَالَتِ امْرَأَتُ عِمْرَنَ
رَبِّ إِنِّي نَذَرْتُ لَكَ
مَا فِي بَطْنِي مُحَرَّرًا فَتَقَبَّلْ مِنِّي
إِنَّكَ أَنتَ السَّمِيعُ الْعَلِيمُ

36. When she was delivered,
She said: "O my Lord!
Behold! I am delivered
Of a female child!"—
And Allah knew best
What she brought forth—[377]
"And no wise is the male
Like the female.[378]
I have named her Mary,
And I commend her
And her offspring
To Thy protection
From the Evil One,
The Rejected."

۞ فَلَمَّا وَضَعَتْهَا
قَالَتْ رَبِّ إِنِّي وَضَعْتُهَا أُنثَى
وَاللَّهُ أَعْلَمُ بِمَا وَضَعَتْ
وَلَيْسَ الذَّكَرُ كَالْأُنثَى
وَإِنِّي سَمَّيْتُهَا مَرْيَمَ وَإِنِّي أُعِيذُهَا بِكَ
وَذُرِّيَّتَهَا مِنَ الشَّيْطَانِ الرَّجِيمِ

37. Right graciously
Did her Lord accept her:
He made her grow
In purity and beauty;
To the care of Zakarīya
Was she assigned.

۞ فَتَقَبَّلَهَا رَبُّهَا
بِقَبُولٍ حَسَنٍ وَأَنبَتَهَا نَبَاتًا حَسَنًا
وَكَفَّلَهَا زَكَرِيَّا

---

375. Now we begin the story of Jesus. As a prelude we have the birth of Mary and the parallel story of John the Baptist, Yaḥyā the son of Zakariya. Yaḥyā's mother Elizabeth was a cousin of Mary the mother of Jesus (Luke 1:36), and therefore John and Jesus were cousins by blood, and there was a spiritual cousinhood in their birth and career. Elizabeth was of the daughters of Aaron (Luke 1:5), of a priestly family which went back to Aaron the brother of Moses and son of 'Imrān. Her husband Zakariya was actually a priest, and her cousin Mary was presumably also of a priestly family. By tradition Mary's mother was called Hannah (in Latin, Anna, and in English, Anne), and her father was called 'Imrān. Hannah is therefore both a descendant of the priestly house of 'Imrān and the wife of 'Imrān,—"a woman of 'Imrān" in a double sense.

376. *Muḥarrar*=freed from all worldly affairs and specially dedicated to Allah's service. She expected a son, who was to be a special devotee, a miraculous son of the old age of his parents, but Allah gave her instead a daughter. But that daughter was Mary the mother of Jesus, the chosen one among the women; 3:42.

377. The mother of Mary expected a male child. Was she disappointed that it was a female child? No, for she had faith, and she knew that Allah's Plan was better than any wishes of hers. Mary was no ordinary girl: only Allah knew what it was that her mother brought forth.

378. The female child could not be devoted to Temple service under the Mosaic law, as she intended. But she was marked out for a special destiny as a miracle-child, to be the mother of the miracle-child Jesus. She was content to seek Allah's protection for her against all evil. There is a certain sense of pride in the girl on the part of the mother.

Every time that he entered
(Her) chamber to see her,
He found her supplied
With sustenance. He said:
"O Mary! Whence (comes) this
To you?" She said:
"From Allah: for Allah
Provides sustenance
To whom He pleases,
Without measure."[379]

كُلَّمَا دَخَلَ عَلَيۡهَا زَكَرِيَّا ٱلۡمِحۡرَابَ

وَجَدَ عِندَهَا رِزۡقًا ۖ قَالَ يَٰمَرۡيَمُ

أَنَّىٰ لَكِ هَٰذَا ۖ قَالَتۡ هُوَ مِنۡ عِندِ ٱللَّهِ

إِنَّ ٱللَّهَ يَرۡزُقُ مَن يَشَآءُ بِغَيۡرِ حِسَابٍ

38. There did Zakarīya
Pray to his Lord, saying:
"O my Lord! Grant unto me
From Thee a progeny
That is pure: for Thou
Art He that heareth prayer!"[380]

﴿٣٨﴾ هُنَالِكَ دَعَا زَكَرِيَّا رَبَّهُۥ ۖ

قَالَ رَبِّ هَبۡ لِي مِن لَّدُنكَ ذُرِّيَّةً

طَيِّبَةً ۖ إِنَّكَ سَمِيعُ ٱلدُّعَآءِ

39. While he was standing
In prayer in the chamber,
The angels called unto him:
"Allah doth give thee
Glad tidings of Yaḥyā,
Witnessing the truth
Of a Word from Allah,[381] and (be
Besides) noble, chaste,
And a Prophet—
Of the (goodly) company
Of the righteous."

﴿٣٩﴾ فَنَادَتۡهُ ٱلۡمَلَٰٓئِكَةُ

وَهُوَ قَآئِمٌ يُصَلِّي فِي ٱلۡمِحۡرَابِ

أَنَّ ٱللَّهَ يُبَشِّرُكَ بِيَحۡيَىٰ مُصَدِّقًۢا

بِكَلِمَةٍ مِّنَ ٱللَّهِ وَسَيِّدًا وَحَصُورًا

وَنَبِيًّا مِّنَ ٱلصَّٰلِحِينَ

40. He said: "Oh my Lord!
How shall I have a son,
Seeing I am very old,
And my wife is barren?"
"Thus," was the answer,
"Doth Allah accomplish
What He willeth."

﴿٤٠﴾ قَالَ رَبِّ أَنَّىٰ يَكُونُ لِي غُلَٰمٌ

وَقَدۡ بَلَغَنِيَ ٱلۡكِبَرُ وَٱمۡرَأَتِي عَاقِرٌ ۖ

قَالَ كَذَٰلِكَ ٱللَّهُ يَفۡعَلُ مَا يَشَآءُ

---

379. Mary grew under Allah's special protection. Her sustenance, under which we may include both her physical needs and her spiritual food, came from Allah, and her growth was indeed a "goodly growth" which I have tried to express in the text by the words "purity and beauty". Some aprocryphal Christian writings say that she was brought up in the Temple to the age of twelve like a dove, and that she was fed by angels.

380. The birth of Mary, the mother of Jesus, of John the Baptist, the precursor of Jesus, and of Jesus, the prophet of Israel, whom Israel rejected, occurred in that order chronologically, and are told in that order. They are all interconnected. Zakariyā prayed for no ordinary son. He and his wife were past the age of parenthood. Seeing the growth of Mary, he prayed for some child from Allah,—"from Thee, a progeny that is pure". Perhaps he had adoption in his mind. Did he want to adopt Mary? To his surprise, he is given a son in the flesh, ushered in by a special Sign. (R).

381. Notice: "*a* Word from Allah", not "*the* Word of Allah", the epithet that mystical Christianity uses for Jesus. As stated in 3:59 below, Jesus was created by a miracle, by Allah's word "Be", and he was.

41. He said: "O my Lord!
Give me a Sign!"
"Thy Sign," was the answer,
"Shall be that thou
Shalt speak to no man
For three days
But with signals.
Then celebrate
The praises of thy Lord
Again and again,
And glorify Him
In the evening
And in the morning."

SECTION 5.

42. Behold! the angels said:
"O Mary! Allah hath chosen
thee
And purified thee—chosen thee
Above the women of all
nations.[382]

43. "O Mary! worship
Thy Lord devoutly:
Prostrate thyself,
And bow down (in prayer)
With those who bow down."

44. This is part of the tidings
Of the things unseen,[383]
Which We reveal unto thee
(O Prophet!) by inspiration:
Thou wast not with them
When they cast lots
With arrows,[384] as to which
Of them should be charged
With the care of Mary:
Nor wast thou with them

---

382. Mary, the mother of Jesus, was unique, in that she gave birth to a son by a special miracle, without the intervention of the customary physical means. This of course does not mean that she was more than human, any more than that her son was more than human. She had as much need to pray to Allah as anyone else. The Christian dogma, in all sects except the Unitarian, holds that Jesus was God and the son of God. The worship of Mary became the practice in the Roman Catholic Church, which calls Mary the "Mother of God". This seems to have been endorsed by the Council of Ephesus in 431 A.C., in the century before Muḥammad was born to sweep away the corruptions of the Church of Christ. For *'ālamīn* as meaning all nations, see 3:96, n. 423.

383. *Things unseen*: belong to a realm beyond the reach of human perception and therefore it would be unseemly to dispute or speculate about them. (R).

384. Literally, *reeds: aqlām*. For the Arab custom of casting lots with arrows, see 2:219, n. 241.

When they disputed (the point).[385]

إِذۡ يَخۡتَصِمُونَ

45. Behold! the angels said:
"O Mary! Allah giveth thee
Glad tidings of a Word
From Him: his name
Will be Christ Jesus.[386]
The son of Mary, held in honour
In this world and the Hereafter
And of (the company of) those
Nearest to Allah;[387]

﴿٤٥﴾ إِذۡ قَالَتِ ٱلۡمَلَـٰٓئِكَةُ
يَـٰمَرۡيَمُ إِنَّ ٱللَّهَ يُبَشِّرُكِ بِكَلِمَةٍ مِّنۡهُ
ٱسۡمُهُ ٱلۡمَسِيحُ عِيسَى ٱبۡنُ مَرۡيَمَ وَجِيهًا
فِى ٱلدُّنۡيَا وَٱلۡأَخِرَةِ وَمِنَ ٱلۡمُقَرَّبِينَ

46. "He shall speak to the people
In craddle and in maturity.[388]
And he shall be (of the company)
Of the righteous."

﴿٤٦﴾ وَيُكَلِّمُ ٱلنَّاسَ فِى ٱلۡمَهۡدِ
وَكَهۡلًا وَمِنَ ٱلصَّـٰلِحِينَ

47. She said: "O my Lord![389]
How shall I have a son
When no man hath touched me?"
He said: "Even so:
Allah createth
What He willeth:
When He hath decreed
A Plan, He but saith
To it, 'Be,' and it is!

﴿٤٧﴾ قَالَتۡ رَبِّ أَنَّىٰ يَكُونُ لِى وَلَدٌ
وَلَمۡ يَمۡسَسۡنِى بَشَرٌ قَالَ كَذَٰلِكِ
ٱللَّهُ يَخۡلُقُ مَا يَشَآءُ إِذَا قَضَىٰٓ أَمۡرًا
فَإِنَّمَا يَقُولُ لَهُۥ كُن فَيَكُونُ

48. "And Allah will teach him
The Book and Wisdom,
The Law and the Gospel,

﴿٤٨﴾ وَيُعَلِّمُهُ ٱلۡكِتَـٰبَ
وَٱلۡحِكۡمَةَ وَٱلتَّوۡرَىٰةَ وَٱلۡإِنجِيلَ

49. "And (appoint him)
A messenger to the Children
Of Israel, (with this message):
'I have come to you,
With a Sign from your Lord,
In that I make for you

﴿٤٩﴾ وَرَسُولًا إِلَىٰ بَنِىٓ إِسۡرَٰٓءِيلَ
أَنِّى قَدۡ جِئۡتُكُم بِـَٔايَةٍ مِّن رَّبِّكُمۡ
أَنِّىٓ أَخۡلُقُ لَكُم

---

385. Christian apocryphal writings mention the contention between the priests as to the honour of taking charge of Mary, and how it was decided by means of rods and reeds in favour of Zakarīya.

386. *Christ:* Greek, *Christos* = anointed: kings and priests were anointed to symbolise consecration to their office. The Hebrew and Arabic form is *Masīḥ*.

387. Nearest to Allah: *Muqarrabīn, Cf.* 56:11.

388. The ministry of Jesus lasted only about three years, from 30 to 33 years of his age, when in the eyes of his enemies he was crucified. But the Gospel of Luke (2:46) describes him as disputing with the doctors in the Temple at the age of 12, and even earlier, as a child, he was "strong in spirit, filled with wisdom" (Luke 2:40).Some apocryphal Gospels describe him as preaching from infancy.

389. She was addressed by angels, who gave her Allah's message. In reply she speaks as to Allah. In reply, apparently an angel again gives Allah's message.

مِنَ الطِّينِ كَهَيْئَةِ الطَّيْرِ

Out of clay,
The figure of a bird,
And breathe into it,
And it becomes a bird
By Allah's leave:[390]
And I heal those
Born blind, and the lepers,
And I quicken the dead,
By Allah's leave;
And I declare to you
What ye eat, and what ye
store[391]
In your houses. Surely
Therein is a Sign for you
If ye did believe;

فَأَنفُخُ فِيهِ فَيَكُونُ طَيْرًا بِإِذْنِ اللَّهِ

وَأُبْرِئُ الْأَكْمَهَ وَالْأَبْرَصَ

وَأُحْيِ الْمَوْتَىٰ بِإِذْنِ اللَّهِ

وَأُنَبِّئُكُم بِمَا تَأْكُلُونَ وَمَا تَدَّخِرُونَ

فِي بُيُوتِكُمْ إِنَّ فِي ذَٰلِكَ لَآيَةً لَّكُمْ

إِن كُنتُم مُّؤْمِنِينَ

50. " '(I have come to you),
To attest the Law
Which was before me.
And to make lawful
To you part of what was
(Before) forbidden to you;
I have come to you
With a Sign from your Lord.
So fear Allah
And obey me.' "

﴿٥٠﴾ وَمُصَدِّقًا لِّمَا بَيْنَ يَدَيَّ مِنَ التَّوْرَاةِ

وَلِأُحِلَّ لَكُم بَعْضَ الَّذِي حُرِّمَ عَلَيْكُمْ

وَجِئْتُكُم بِآيَةٍ مِّن رَّبِّكُمْ

فَاتَّقُوا اللَّهَ وَأَطِيعُونِ

51. " 'It is Allah
Who is my Lord
And your Lord;
Then worship Him.
This is a Way
That is straight.' "

﴿٥١﴾ إِنَّ اللَّهَ رَبِّي

وَرَبُّكُمْ فَاعْبُدُوهُ

هَٰذَا صِرَاطٌ مُّسْتَقِيمٌ

52. When Jesus found
Unbelief on their part
He said: "Who will be
My helpers to (the work
Of) Allah?" Said the Disciples:
"We are Allah's helpers:
We believe in Allah,

﴿٥٢﴾ فَلَمَّا أَحَسَّ عِيسَىٰ مِنْهُمُ الْكُفْرَ

قَالَ مَنْ أَنصَارِي إِلَى اللَّهِ قَالَ الْحَوَارِيُّونَ

نَحْنُ أَنصَارُ اللَّهِ آمَنَّا بِاللَّهِ

---

390. This miracle of the clay birds is found in some of the apocryphal Gospels; those of curing the blind and the lepers and raising the dead are in the canonical Gospels. The original Gospel (see 3:48) was not the various stories written afterwards by disciples, but the real Message taught direct by Jesus.

391. I do not know whether this clause refers to a particular incident, or generally to a prophetic knowledge of what is not known to ordinary people.

And do thou bear witness
That we are Muslims.[392]

وَٱشْهَدْ بِأَنَّا مُسْلِمُونَ

53. "Our Lord! we believe
In what Thou hast revealed,
And we follow the Messenger;
Then write us down
Among those who bear witness."

۞ رَبَّنَآ ءَامَنَّا بِمَآ أَنزَلْتَ وَٱتَّبَعْنَا ٱلرَّسُولَ فَٱكْتُبْنَا مَعَ ٱلشَّٰهِدِينَ

54 And (the unbelievers)
Plotted and planned,
And Allah too planned,[393]
And the best of planners
Is Allah.

۞ وَمَكَرُواْ وَمَكَرَ ٱللَّهُ وَٱللَّهُ خَيْرُ ٱلْمَٰكِرِينَ

SECTION 6.

55. Behold! Allah said:
"O Jesus! I will take thee[394]
And raise thee to Myself
And clear thee (of the
falsehoods)[395]
Of those who blaspheme;
I will make those
Who follow thee superior[396]
To those who reject faith,
To the Day of Resurrection:
Then shall ye all
Return unto me,
And I will judge
Between you of the matters
Wherein ye dispute.[397]

۞ إِذْ قَالَ ٱللَّهُ يَٰعِيسَىٰٓ إِنِّى مُتَوَفِّيكَ وَرَافِعُكَ إِلَىَّ وَمُطَهِّرُكَ مِنَ ٱلَّذِينَ كَفَرُواْ وَجَاعِلُ ٱلَّذِينَ ٱتَّبَعُوكَ فَوْقَ ٱلَّذِينَ كَفَرُوٓاْ إِلَىٰ يَوْمِ ٱلْقِيَٰمَةِ ثُمَّ إِلَىَّ مَرْجِعُكُمْ فَأَحْكُمُ بَيْنَكُمْ فِيمَا كُنتُمْ فِيهِ تَخْتَلِفُونَ

392. (*Cf.* 5:11) The story of Jesus is told with special application to the time of the Prophet Muḥammad. Note the word helpers (*Anṣār*) in this connection, and the reference to plotters in 3:54. It was the one Religion — the Religion of Allah, which was in essence the religion of Abraham, Moses, and Jesus. The argument runs: who do ye then now make divisions and reject the living Teacher? Islam is: bowing to the Will of Allah. All who have faith should bow to the Will of Allah and be Muslims.

393. The Arabic *makara* has both a bad and a good meaning, that of making an intricate plan to carry out some secret purpose. The enemies of Allah are constantly doing that. But Allah — in whose hands is all good — has His plans also, against which the evil ones will have no chance whatever (*Cf.* 8:30, 13:42, and 27:50).

394. Read this with 4:157-158, where it is said that "whereas they slew him not nor they crucified him but it was made dubious unto". The guilt of the Jews remained, but Jesus was eventually taken up to Allah.

395. Jesus was charged by the Jews with blasphemy as claiming to be God or the son of God. The Christians (except a few early sects which were annihilated by persecution, and the modern sect of Unitarians), adopted the substance of the claim, and made it the cornerstone of their faith. Allah clears Jesus of such a charge or claim.

396. *Those who follow thee* refers to both Muslims (insofar as they truly follow the basic teachings of Jesus) and Christians (who claim to follow him). [Eds.].

397. All the controversies about dogma and faith will disappear when we appear before Allah. He will judge not by what we profess but by what we are.

56. "As to those who reject faith,
I will punish them
With terrible agony
In this world and in the
                 Hereafter,
Nor will they have
Anyone to help.

57. "As to those who believe
And work righteousness,
Allah will pay them (in full)
Their reward:
But Allah loveth not
Those who do wrong.

58. "This is what we rehearse
Unto thee of the Signs
And the Message
Of Wisdom."

59. The similitude of Jesus
Before Allah is as that of
                Adam;[398]
He created him from dust,
Then said to him: "Be":
And he was.

60. The Truth (comes)
From thy Lord alone;
So be not of those
Who doubt.[399]

61. If anyone disputes
In this matter with thee,
Now after (full) knowledge
Hath come to thee,
Say: "Come! let us
Gather together—
Our sons and your sons,
Our women and your women,
Ourselves and yourselves:
Then let us earnestly pray,

---

398. After a description of the high position which Jesus occupies as a prophet, we have a repudiation of the dogma that he was Allah, or the son of Allah, or anything more than a man. If it is said that he was born without a human father, Adam was also so born. Indeed Adam was born without either a human father or mother. As far as our physical bodies are concerned they are mere dust. In Allah's sight Jesus was as dust just as Adam was or humanity is. The greatness of Jesus arose from the Divine command "Be": for after that he was—more than dust—a great spiritual leader and teacher.

399. The truth does not necessarily come from priests, or from the superstitions of whole peoples. It comes from Allah, and where there is a direct revelation, there is no room for doubt (*Cf.* 10:94).

And invoke the curse
Of Allah on those who lie!"[400]

فَنَجْعَل لَّعْنَتَ ٱللَّهِ عَلَى ٱلْكَٰذِبِينَ

62. This is the true account;[401]
There is no god
Except Allah;
And Allah—He is indeed
The Exalted in Power,
The Wise.

﴿٦٢﴾ إِنَّ هَٰذَا لَهُوَ ٱلْقَصَصُ ٱلْحَقُّ
وَمَا مِنْ إِلَٰهٍ إِلَّا ٱللَّهُ وَإِنَّ ٱللَّهَ لَهُوَ
ٱلْعَزِيزُ ٱلْحَكِيمُ

63. But if they turn back,
Allah hath full knowledge
Of those who do mischief.

﴿٦٣﴾ فَإِن تَوَلَّوْا فَإِنَّ ٱللَّهَ عَلِيمٌۢ بِٱلْمُفْسِدِينَ

C. 57.—Islam doth invite all people
(3:64-120.)   To the Truth; there is no cause
For dissembling or disputing.
False are the people who corrupt
Allah's truth, or hinder men
From coming to Allah. Let the Muslims
Hold together in unity and discipline,
Knowing that they have a mission
Of righteousness for humanity.
No harm can come to them.
Though there are good men and true
In other Faiths, Muslims must
Be true to their own Brotherhood.
They should seek help and friendship
From their own, and stand firm
In constancy and patient perseverance.

---

400. In the year of Deputations, 10th of the Hijrah, came a Christian embassy from Najrān (towards Yaman, about 150 miles north of Ṣan'ā). They were much impressed on hearing this passage of the Qur'ān explaining the true position of Christ, and they entered into tributary relations with the new Muslim State. But ingrained habits and customs prevented them from accepting Islam as a body. The Holy Prophet, firm in his faith, proposed a *Mubāhalah, i.e.,* a solemn meeting, in which both sides should summon not only their men, but their women and children, earnestly pray to Allah, and invoke the curse of Allah on those who should lie. Those who had a pure and sincere faith would not hesitate. The Christians declined, and they were dismissed in a spirit of tolerance with a promise of protection from the State in return for tribute, "the wages of rule," as it is called in the *Āīni Akbarī.*

401. We are now in a position to deal with the questions which we left over at 2:87, Jesus is no more than a man. It is against reason and revelation to call him God or the son of God. He is called the son of Mary to emphasise this. He had no human father, as his birth was miraculous. But it was not this which raised him to his high spiritual position as a prophet, but because Allah called him to his office. The praise is due to Allah, Who by His word gave him spiritual strength—"strengthened him with the holy spirit." The miracles which surround his story relate not only to his birth and his life and death, but also to his mother Mary and his precursor Yaḥyā. These were the "Clear Signs" which he brought. It was those who misunderstood him who obscured his clear Signs and surrounded him with mysteries of their own invention. (R).

SECTION 7.

64. Say: "O People
Of the Book! come
To common terms
As between us and you:
That we worship
None but Allah;
That we associate
No partners with Him;
That we erect not,
From among ourselves,
Lords and patrons
Other than Allah."[402]
If then they turn back,
Say ye: "Bear witness
That we (at least)
Are Muslims (bowing
To Allah's Will)."

٦٤ ۞ قُل يَٰٓأَهْلَ ٱلْكِتَٰبِ تَعَالَوْا۟
إِلَىٰ كَلِمَةٍ سَوَآءٍۭ بَيْنَنَا وَبَيْنَكُمْ
أَلَّا نَعْبُدَ إِلَّا ٱللَّهَ وَلَا نُشْرِكَ بِهِۦ
شَيْـًٔا وَلَا يَتَّخِذَ بَعْضُنَا
بَعْضًا أَرْبَابًا مِّن دُونِ ٱللَّهِ
فَإِن تَوَلَّوْا۟ فَقُولُوا۟
ٱشْهَدُوا۟ بِأَنَّا
مُسْلِمُونَ

65. Ye People of the Book!
Why dispute ye
About Abraham,
When the Law and the Gospel
Were not revealed
Till after him?
Have ye no understanding?

٦٥ ۞ يَٰٓأَهْلَ ٱلْكِتَٰبِ لِمَ تُحَآجُّونَ فِىٓ
إِبْرَٰهِيمَ وَمَآ أُنزِلَتِ ٱلتَّوْرَىٰةُ وَٱلْإِنجِيلُ
إِلَّا مِنۢ بَعْدِهِۦٓ أَفَلَا تَعْقِلُونَ

66. Ah! Ye are those
Who fell to disputing
(Even) in matters of which
Ye had some knowledge![403]
But why dispute ye
In matters of which
Ye have no knowledge?
It is Allah Who knows,
And ye who know not!

٦٦ ۞ هَٰٓأَنتُمْ هَٰٓؤُلَآءِ حَٰجَجْتُمْ
فِيمَا لَكُم بِهِۦ عِلْمٌ فَلِمَ تُحَآجُّونَ
فِيمَا لَيْسَ لَكُم بِهِۦ عِلْمٌ
وَٱللَّهُ يَعْلَمُ وَأَنتُمْ لَا تَعْلَمُونَ

---

402. In the abstract the People of the Book would agree to all three propositions. In practice they fail. Apart from doctrinal lapses from the unity of the One True God, there is the question of a consecrated Priesthood (among the Jews it was hereditary also), as if a mere human being—Cohen, or Pope, or Priest, or Brahman—could claim superiority apart from his learning and the purity of his life, or could stand between man and Allah in some special sense. The same remarks apply to the worship of saints. They may be pure and holy, but no one can protect us or claim Lordship over us except Allah. For *Rabb*, see 1:2, n. 20. Abraham was a true man of God, but he could not be called a Jew or a Christian as he lived long before the Law of Moses or the Gospel of Jesus was revealed.

403. The number of sects among the Jews and Christians shows that they wrangled and disputed even about some of the matters of their own religion, of which they should have had some knowledge. But when they talk of Father Abraham, they are entirely out of court, as he lived before their peculiar systems were evolved.

67. Abraham was not a Jew
Nor yet a Christian;
But he was true in Faith,
And bowed his will to Allah's,
(Which is Islam),
And he joined not gods with
Allah.[404]

٦٧ مَا كَانَ إِبْرَٰهِيمُ يَهُودِيًّا وَلَا نَصْرَانِيًّا
وَلَٰكِن كَانَ حَنِيفًا مُّسْلِمًا
وَمَا كَانَ مِنَ ٱلْمُشْرِكِينَ

68. Without a doubt, among men,
The nearest of kin to Abraham,
Are those who follow him,
As are also this Prophet
And those who believe:
And Allah is the Protector
Of those who have faith.

٦٨ إِنَّ أَوْلَى ٱلنَّاسِ بِإِبْرَٰهِيمَ
لَلَّذِينَ ٱتَّبَعُوهُ وَهَٰذَا ٱلنَّبِىُّ وَٱلَّذِينَ ءَامَنُوا
وَٱللَّهُ وَلِيُّ ٱلْمُؤْمِنِينَ

69. It is the wish of a section
Of the People of the Book
To lead you astray.
But they shall lead astray
(Not you), but themselves,
And they do not perceive!

٦٩ وَدَّت طَّآئِفَةٌ مِّنْ أَهْلِ ٱلْكِتَٰبِ
لَوْ يُضِلُّونَكُمْ وَمَا يُضِلُّونَ إِلَّآ أَنفُسَهُمْ
وَمَا يَشْعُرُونَ

70. Ye People of the Book!
Why reject ye
The Signs of Allah,
Of which ye are
(Yourselves) witnesses?

٧٠ يَٰٓأَهْلَ ٱلْكِتَٰبِ لِمَ تَكْفُرُونَ
بِـَٔايَٰتِ ٱللَّهِ وَأَنتُمْ تَشْهَدُونَ

71. Ye People of the Book!
Why do ye clothe
Truth with falsehood,
And conceal the Truth,
While ye have knowledge?[405]

٧١ يَٰٓأَهْلَ ٱلْكِتَٰبِ لِمَ تَلْبِسُونَ ٱلْحَقَّ
بِٱلْبَٰطِلِ وَتَكْتُمُونَ ٱلْحَقَّ وَأَنتُمْ تَعْلَمُونَ

* Sūrah Al-Imrān consists of
200 verses. Only a portion
of the surah is presented here.

404. Cf. 2:135 and the whole argument in that passage.

405. There are many ways of preventing the access of people to the truth. One is to tamper with it, or trick it out in colours of falsehood: half-truths are often more dangerous than obvious falsehoods. Another is to conceal it altogether. Those who are jealous of a prophet of Allah, whom they actually see before them, do not allow his credentials or virtues to be known, or vilify him, or conceal facts which would attract people to him. When people do this of set purpose, against their own light ("of which ye are yourselves witnesses"), they are descending to the lowest depths of degradation, and they are doing more harm to themselves than to anyone else. (R).

Suggested Readings

For further reading about Jesus, Mary and Christianity, refer:

1. 'Abdullah Yūsuf 'Alī, *The Meaning of the Holy Qur'ān: New Edition with Revised Translation and Commentary,* amana publications, 1994. The following *sūrahs* and verses in the original work:

Christians, 2: 111; 2: 113; 2: 120; 2: 135; 5: 14; 5: 18;
        Appendix III, p. 291; 22:17; n. 5448
        believers rewarded, 2: 62; 5: 69; 5: 85; 57: 27-29

Jesus

        and the Holy Spirit, 2: 87; 2: 253; 5: 110; 21: 90
        annunciation of, 3: 45-51; 19: 16-21
        a sign, 21: 90; 23: 50; 43: 57-61
        belief in, 4: 159
        covenant with Allah, 33: 7
        cursed the Children of Israel, 5: 78
        Disciples of, 3: 52-54; 5: 111-113; 57: 27; 61: 14
        given the revelation, 2: 87; 2: 136; 2: 253; 3: 48; 3: 84; 4: 163;
            5: 46; 19: 30; 57: 27
        gives glad tidings of Ahmad, 61: 6
        in the ranks of the Righteous, 6: 85
        is not Allah, 5: 17; 5: 72; 9: 30-31
        like Adam, 3: 59
        Messenger to Israel, 3: 49-51; 5: 46; 5: 72; 43: 59; 61: 6; 61: 14
        miracles of, 5: 110; 5: 113-115
        no more than a Messenger, 4: 171; 5: 75; 43: 59
        raised to Allah, 3: 55; 4: 158
        religion of, 42: 13
        serves Allah, 4: 172; 19: 30; 43: 64
        spoke in infancy, 3: 46; 5: 110; 19: 30-33
        testifies before Allah, 5: 116-118
        was not killed, 4: 157; 5: 110
        Wisdom of, 43: 63

2. Haykal, Muhammad Husayn, *The Life of Muhammad*, translated from the 8th edition by Isma'il R. A. al Faruqi, North American Trust Publications, 1976.

3. Kamel Mustafa Hallak, *El Corán Sagrado y la traducción de su sentido en lengua española*, amana publications, 1998.

4. Jeffrey Lang, *Struggling to Surrender: Some Impressions of an American Convert to Islam*, amana publications, 1994.

5. Jeffrey Lang, *Even Angels Ask: A Journey to Islam in America*, amana publications, 1997.

6. Dirks, Jerald, *The Cross & The Crescent –An Interfaith Dialogue between Christianity and Islam*, amana publications, 2001.